Blanket Stories

Blanket Stories

**Richard Jochum and
Ruth Zamoyta, Editors**

Ragged Sky Press
Princeton, New Jersey

Copyright © 2014 by Ragged Sky Press
Introduction copyright © 2014 by Dorothea Lasky

All rights reserved under International and Pan-American Copyright Conventions.

Published by Ragged Sky Press
PO Box 312
Annandale, NJ 08801

ISBN 978-1-933974-13-2
Library of Congress Control Number 2014939239

A list of acknowledgments appears in the back of this book.

Cover Art: "Widow's Quilt" by Mariella Bisson, photo by Nancy Donskoj
Copyright © by Mariella Bisson; used by permission

Cover and interior design by John Figurski

This book is composed in Adobe® Caslon™ Pro and Neue Helvetica®.

raggedsky.com

Manufactured in the United States of America
First Edition

to our siblings

Table of Contents

ix	*Preface by Richard Jochum*
xi	*Introduction by Dorothea Lasky*
3	Christopher Woods, "stay"
5	David Breeden, "Shreds"
6	Jennifer Arin, "The Origin of Peace"
7	Ellen Foos, "Happily Ever After"
9	Dean Kostos, "The Loom Canoe"
10	Maria Terrone, "The Castle"
12	Austin Alexis, "Grace"
13	Susan Laughter Meyers, "Blankets, a Childhood"
15	Michelle Young, "The Pied Piper"
17	Ruth Zamoyta, "Under the Blanket"
18	Zara Raab, "Goldilocks"
20	Dawn Ferchak, " 'And the little one said…'"
22	Enriqueta Carrington, "On Stealing Figs"
24	David Macpherson, "The Five Senses at the Fair"
26	Janelle Adsit, "Introduction to World Peace, Course Final"
28	B.T. Joy, "Our Vision"
30	Nicole Callihan, "The Prayer"
32	Michael Smolinsky, "To My Younger Brother at a Zen Monastery"
34	Brittany Ericksen, "Firstborn"
35	Lois Marie Harrod, "Barbara"
36	Dawn Corrigan, "The Pair Who Stayed"
38	Nancy Cook, "One Sixth"
39	Juditha Dowd, "I Assume the Duties of the Eldest Child"
41	Jacqueline Hughes Simon, "Cut to Measure"
42	Roslyn Tanner Evans, "If Only"
43	Gail Denham, "So Many Years"
44	Anne Harding Woodworth, "Landays for a Drunk"
46	John A. Vanek, "Heavenly Father, help me"
48	Isabalino Anastasio Guzman, "My Grandfather's Blanket"

Table of Contents *continued*

50	Rosemary O'Neil Wright, "Harmony"
52	Sherri Lynn Cooper, "The Blanket"
53	Judith McNally, "Blanket"
55	Manhattanpoet, "The Blanket"
56	Lisa Lebduska, "Butterfly Sleep"
58	Sharon Olson, "Looking for My Other Brother"
59	Carolyn Faye Davis, "The Blanket"
61	Basil Rouskas, "Shared Blanket"
63	*Poet Biographies*
72	*Artist Biographies*
73	*Acknowledgments*

Illustrations

4	Juyoung Yoo, "There's power in a tug."
8	Juyoung Yoo, "The loom cradled us, a canoe."
11	Rebecca Bersohn, "Build no walls within…"
14	Juyoung Yoo, "The piper blew his horn…"
16	John Figurski, "Under Cover"
19	Juyoung Yoo, "Well, that was long ago and far away."
21	Cecilia Oh, "There were always spaces to wriggle into…"
25	Juyoung Yoo, "The blanket was big and warm and felt like soft creation…"
31	John Figurski, "The Sleeping Blonde"
33	Rebecca Bersohn, "Was I cruel, anxious, caught off guard?"
37	John Figurski, "Who's Driving?"
40	Juyoung Yoo, "Cut to measure, as a candy bar to kids…"
45	John Figurski, "The Wild Bunch"
47	Juyoung Yoo, "Help me get up off my knees, sweep him into my arms…"
51	Rebecca Bersohn, "Then somebody starts to sing."
54	Juyoung Yoo, "All we can do is hang on to our pendulum…"
57	Cecilia Oh, "The long nap that erupts us…"
60	Juyoung Yoo, "In tattered clothes be our garment."

Preface

This is the story of a blanket. . . . Once upon a time, there was a great man and his lovely wife and they had five fine children. They raised them with all their love, took good care of them, and as they grew older, they put together a will to continue their support. Apart from their wealth they left them a big warm blanket for the cold winter days. The five children were happy to have a blanket and took it to cover themselves as the days grew colder. One day, as they were lying under the blanket, two of them felt their feet sticking out and got cold around their toes. So, they pulled at the blanket to cover their feet. But now, two of the brothers on the other side of the blanket felt a chill around their feet and so they started to tug back. This went back and forth, back and forth, a number of times, till two of them got up, being annoyed, and decided to leave their three siblings in search for their own blankets. They did not understand that the blanket was big enough to cover them all, if only they had come a little closer towards each other.

Blanket Stories is based on a short story inspired by the tales and fables of La Fontaine and Aesop. Their moral teachings through parables and animal stories have captivated me since I was a child. And although the constellation, five siblings squabbling over stuff, is personal to me and reflects how I grew up, it is the universal application that makes the story powerful. Fables are universal because they tell stories about things that we have in common, in a form that is clear and compelling, no treatises needed. By giving us a way to express the common thread of humanity, they weave the fabric of the social, connect us, and build societies from crowds.

The story of a blanket rests on a simple insight: Blankets are always too small. No matter how big, they will always cover only a part, and, if we pull on them, expose previously covered parts. Blanket Stories is based on the fact that every blanket is limited and will never shield the whole. I sometimes bring a blanket to my classes and tell students that theories, no matter how potent or seductive, are like blankets: they cover parts and expose others. There will always be squabbles, grievances, and feet sticking out. This applies to schools of thought as much as to people.

The passing of parents often makes siblings, now adults, become children again, and reinstalls their childhood rivalries. In the absence of their parents, they have to reposition themselves. In this way, Blanket Stories is about relationships. It makes us reflect how we relate to each other and the value, challenge, fortunate possibility, and unfortunate impossibility of community in relation to the individual. Each of us inherits a role even before we earn it. Mine, for example, was the role of a mediator, and I didn't even understand that, until my father's passing.

Preface *continued*

Blankets prevent us from getting cold. But they also provide comfort. For many children, as they grow up, blankets represent security as much as they do warmth. Developmental psychologists have called them transitional or transformational objects, ideal to make children probe their relationship with the world. It is its ability to hold many meanings which makes the story of a blanket a suitable gateway for our imagination, thus turning a single story into *blanket stories*.

I understand art as a form of education, and the tale as a particularly compelling form, due to its innate ability to cut to the chase. Because of its simplicity, it seems to provide a perfect tool for teaching. However, the simplicity is both a strength and a pitfall. A tale usually ends with a conclusion that summarizes the moral of the story. Despite the value of the tale, the moral ending always seemed problematic to me; it imposes one interpretation and ousts other points of view. This is why I invited poets and visual artists to interpret the story of the blanket in their own ways. Blanket Stories was created as an open call to poets and visual artists to enrich the story with multiple perspectives and bring to it the full diversity of human experience. By exposing a simple, narrated tale to many artistic reiterations, the message is refracted through multiple lenses. Every poem becomes a way to contest the overall morality of the tale and opens it up for discussion and reassessment.

By soliciting various viewpoints, Blanket Stories has become a collaborative project involving more than one hundred poets, artists, and performers. While some of the outcome has been published in this book, additional content can be found online at *blanketstories.net*. The goal is to demonstrate how the significance of a parable can be personally grasped and poetically reiterated or extrapolated in an infinite number of creative ways while being used to collaborate and for teaching.

Our hope for this project is to increase appreciation for and understanding of poetry. Poems can be intimidating when we have no point of reference. We often don't know how to read them or what the poet was thinking. Because the tale of the blanket is a template used by all poets in this book, the reader can look to the story as a starting point for interpreting the poems and understanding how poets use language to express meaning.

Richard Jochum
New York, May 2014

An Introduction to Collaboration and the Celebration of the Blanket

It is such an honor to write the introduction for this book and to be part of this project, the creation of the brilliant and otherworldly Richard Jochum. Richard envisioned such an incredible platform for writers and artists to collaborate across genres for this book—the story of a blanket that is too small for a group of siblings, who in their struggle to get their own space, realize only when it is almost too late that the blanket becomes bigger the closer they are together.

It is a wonderful story not only about family, but also about collaboration. When people collaborate artistically, it is so important not to have each ego overwhelm the larger goal. Many times this is where the idea of compromise comes in—each person must concede to any stubborn notions and do what is best for the overall project. They must submerge the ego to the group ego and to the health of whatever it is they are creating.

Blankets have a special familial connotation for me, because my mother, who is a professor of Native American art, adorned our walls with many brightly colored blankets from all over the country. Our family room was painted a dark russet, the perfect complement to the sparkling red, grey, yellow, purple, green, orange, and cream tones of our biggest eye-dazzlers. For me, blankets have always been about beauty and the grace of the art object, and not always about just practical warmth.

Because I grew up putting blankets on the walls, as an adult I followed this practice, too. A special blanket my mother gave me a few years ago is my End of the Day blanket which I keep above my bed. The scene on the blanket is a purple and orange sunset. There is a man on a horse in front of the sunset, his head bent over as he labors to keep awake as his trusted friend takes him home. As I go to sleep each night, the man reminds me of myself, a weary being who will be cured by sleep, ready to face each new day and ride into a scene of sun.

The Blanket Stories project allowed poets to imagine what blankets meant to them and this book is full of pages and pages of beautiful poetry inspired by the project. The sheer magnitude in the book, as well as the web journal, allows us to see just what a generative story it is and one that could be the focal point to many future poems, stories, essays, pictures, films, textile creations, and more.

One poem that was created for this book that has stuck with me is B.T. Joy's piece, "Our Vision." The poem begins telling and retelling a story of beauty, of

An Introduction *continued*

a landscape of everyday wonder, of "purple geraniums" and frolicking "Friesian horses," and lovers who learn about themselves the closer they get to one another. The message of the poem is outward, as it begs the reader and a multitude of readers to consider what violence does to disconnect the human soul from all that is living around it. It suggests that those who sanction and commit the horrible atrocities of war might consider again not only that it is the beauty of "Friesian horses" that they destroy when they fight, but also that the instinct of the horses to play together is an act of collaboration. The final "vision" of the poem is about recalibrating one's own perspective—to see the struggle not just of the self but of all living beings—to have not *my* vision, but *all* vision.

Another poem that struck me in the collection is David Breeden's "Shreds." The short piece tells the story of a blanket bitten to bits, as "all the teeth of empire" exist in the call of " 'It's mine.' And mine. / And mine." By the end of the poem, the pieces of blanket, useless as a heap of scraps, scream that they are not "mine," but "ours." The poem has a similar message to Joy's poem above—that the Blanket Story tells us the more we struggle, the narrower our perspectives will be and that living is about finding out *our* vision and *our* blanket. Breeden's and Joy's poems let us see that we must have a vision of the larger good in order to all be safe, warm, and secure.

A third poem I loved was Michelle Young's poem "The Pied Piper." This poem retells the story of The Pied Piper of Hamelin, who was hired to use his magic pipe to lure the rats away from the town. When the town refused to pay him, he used his pipe to trick the children of the town to walk right out of it with him, never to return. In Young's poem, the persona takes the perspective of one of the children, being led away as "[l]ullabies" turned into "symphonies," all of the children "dancing" together away from their homes, "[t]ossing sparkles as confetti." She describes the town as a "*Neverland,*" one of innocence and perfumed by the "scent of cotton candy," that together as one dancing thing all adults turn themselves away from. At the end of the poem, the persona sings a song of deliverance, telling the reader that despite being away from her home, she has a "secret map" to take them all back to this blissful land, a place of memory and wonder.

The Blanket Story is a story of collaboration and it makes me think of a project I used to do with my K-5 painting and drawing students many years ago in an art center in the suburbs of Boston. The classes I taught were usually a week in length and involved some specific theme to create lessons around, like Outer Space, the Ocean, and Monsters.

An Introduction *continued*

At the end of the week, I would have my students create a large quilt together. I used to be obsessed with using felt in the classroom and I would painstakingly cut felt squares in the exact same dimensions for each student. Then I would provide felt scraps and glue and have the students decorate their own squares with the particular themes in mind. After these were dry, as a class, we would hole-punch all of the squares and use neon-colored yarns to tie the squares together. At the end of the day, we would have a large quilt that I would hang in the hall to represent our class. I would tell my students, *Just look at what we can create when we work together*, and we would all feel very proud.

The Blanket Story also makes me think of a growing collaboration I have with a poet and textile artist, Maria Damon. Recently, Maria wove me a blanket on her loom. The whole process of her making the blanket for me was collaborative, as she had me visit her loom one Sunday afternoon so we could pick out the colors together. I chose so many versions of orange, as of late I have been obsessed with the shade and wanted a celebration of the colors of the sun. She included some pinks, mustards, and dark red in the mix, and I selected some yarn in cool colors to, as I described, "change the vibrations of the oranges."

Several weeks later, Maria wrote me that she was done with the blanket. I went to go see it and was amazed and delighted by it. It contained several kinds of stitches and was orange, mustard, red, russet, marigold, tangerine, pumpkin, pink, gold, and more. It had large pools of green-blue tufts everywhere that she had woven in that looked like a monster's furry head was peeking through.

It was magical and I felt as if we had made it together. She named it "Solar Riot."

The next step will be for me to write a poem inspired by the blanket, which will hopefully be part of a future exhibition of Maria's blankets and poems.

The lesson of this book is that we can all work together, if we want to. There need to be more books like this one, where we collaborate across fields. Oftentimes, art fields keep themselves quarantined, never venturing out far enough into other territories, and, all the while, keeping their vision narrow. Poetry can be a big offender of this, as poetry keeps to itself too much, grumbling about being maligned and small in the larger society, and fights within itself, a bunch of word-loving, spell-casting siblings tearing at what they perceive as the tiny blanket they all share.

I think the key to poetry's future is to get closer together and realize how big the blanket of language is that is wrapping around us.

An Introduction *continued*

This, I believe, is the key to health and growth of all art forms. We need to get closer together within our fields and then get closer together across fields. We need to collaborate with non-artists and see that aesthetic logic is part of any kind of thinking. We need to make a vision of our existence that is large and vast and not trapped by the process of tugging at a blanket.

And like this book asserts by its presence and magnificent work, we need to just do it. So, start a collaboration today. Not only will you create something new and see how beautiful the world is on a grand scale, but you will learn just how fantastically intertwined we all are.

To our blankets and beyond!

Dorothea Lasky
New York, May 2014

Blanket Stories

Christopher Woods

stay

when we are all here
we are far from the world
where anything can happen

when we are here
we breathe each other's breath
touch what binds us

if we leave all this
we could be lost
might be doomed

so we stay for now
but we are growing
larger than we once were

we are running out of blanket
our limbs reach out to sky
to roads that lead away

best to stay if we can
better to stay asleep
dream of being small again.

Juyoung Yoo, *"There's power in a tug."*

David Breeden

Shreds

There's power in a tug.
There's violence in a

pulling away. There's
all the teeth of empire in

"It's mine." And mine.
And mine. The shreds,

the screaming, are ours.

Jennifer Arin

The Origin of Peace

Peace comes to us
not from the ravages
of war, but from
a conquering tongue—
the Normans' French
pes usurping the English
sibb, kindred to our
siblings. Five brothers
once upon a time shared
a blanket fit for them
all, and for the winter
ahead. Yet needless
or maybe heedless tension
crept in, this one's foot sticking
out, that one's toes poking
daftly into the cold, close-
knit kin in the end
unentwining. No peace
without appeasement, no
pax without a pact, no story
without conflict unless
we heed a poem from that
once-conquered country, let
its copiousness cover us
like a blanket: "Stay . . .
till the Tempest cease;
And the loud winds
are lulled into a peace."

Quote from John Dryden, "Dido to Aeneas."

Ellen Foos

Happily Ever After

We several siblings pulled together most of the time,
in one bedroom at first and then spread out into two.
Nighttime reading held us dangling over the edge of sleep.

We knew Peter Rabbit was disobedient and paid dearly.
The five Chinese brothers got busted for taking a chance.
These seemed to us like unfair deals,
while we fought and scrapped
for our rightful amount of cookies or covers.

Our nuns also told moral tales and would have us
pray to enter the biggest fairy kingdom of them all;
the blanket large, the stories no longer punishing.

Juyoung Yoo, *"The loom cradled us, a canoe."*

Dean Kostos

The Loom Canoe

The Navajo believe that a flaw allows the spirit of the blanket to have the freedom to roam and for the blanket to never end.

The mother of all spiders taught our mothers
     to weave. The weft of song passed
          through the warp of breathing, one
               continuous yarn.

When First Man and First Woman rose
     from the underworld, they planted
          soles on soil—night sky
               a flaming lake.

First Woman built a loom with rays
     & rock crystal, hammered with lightning bolts.
          The loom cradled us,
               a canoe. Our sway

wove whorls, our chants purpling wool.
     While fingers plucked threads, the shaman's
          yowl coaxed Buffalo to thunder,
               mountains woven in a zigzag

of black & red. Rain fringed banks
     of the arroyo. The blanket began to weave
          itself, bleeding brown
               & mulberry into sand.

Sawing mouth-bows, gods gnashed the sun.
     Rays slanted: sumac & arrow weed,
          corn pollen & oxblood.
               After ferrying our ghosts

to the watery underworld, the loom canoe sailed
     back to the house of our wound,
          our flaw. The door was the shaman's
               maw, chanting lives into pattern.

Maria Terrone

The Castle

Erase the line drawn in the sand, a scar
old and deep. Shuffle back and forth,

pairs of feet like wheels churning up
clouds. Move hand in hand laughing,

as children do. If you can't decode
the swirl of tongues, hold the hands

tighter. Share water and tools—
now erect a sand castle. Let it be

strong, beautiful, visible for miles.
Build no walls within, unfurl

no flags. Ban the monster-teeming
moat. Instead, create a path for pilgrims

to tread without fear of sudden,
violent death. Make yourself small

so that you can live in the home
you have made. Greet all guests

from the always-unlocked doors,
opening wide. At nightfall, light

a torch at every turret, far
from history's merciless tides.

Rebecca Bersohn, *"Build no walls within..."*

Austin Alexis

Grace

Our hands tackle each other.
They do not know grace
in any of its meanings.
They batter over the blanket
that joins and divides us.
We grip and tug the thick warm thing.
Each of us wants sole ownership.
Each of us sees no "us"
but only an "I,"
an ego afraid of the cold
without the quilt our mother gave to us.

During our din and altercation she appears,
just like a saint in a medieval painting
or a blue-hued Madonna—ethereal.
She's all stained-glass color
and with her hymn-tone voice she implores.
It's peace she desires—*pax, pace,* whatever—
our dear, deceased mother,
alive, a live hallucination,
the imagined abruptly real.

The blanket drops from our hands.
Our fingers clasp each other's
in fright, in prayer,
in a communion of shame and forgiveness.
The next day, our outstretched arms
offer the blanket to a homeless man
we've known for eons
who huddles in doorways
and peacefully waits for blessings.

Susan Laughter Meyers

Blankets, a Childhood

The deep-olive wool one
we called the Army blanket
because it was. I loved its heft,
its official smell. Not mine,
it knew cots & hard ground.
What it knew best: the mystery
of my brother & his crew cut,
absent boy who said so little.

The tan one with two stripes
at the top, coral & turquoise,
we called the Indian blanket.
Dream catcher, exotic & pilled.
Always doubled, folded in half
longways, saying itself twice.
Rolled up, a sister's pillow
when the day went wrong.

My favorite had no name. Faded
red-and-black-checkered cotton
smelling of lotion & salt air.
Sunbather, limp & napless—
the one whose bed was sand.
The sea's dull handkerchief
we gripped the corners of at dusk
& shook, hard, in the devil wind.

Juyoung Yoo, *"The piper blew his horn…"*

Michelle Young

The Pied Piper

       Lost
While we gamboled about
Circles closing opening
In tidal rhythms
              Lullabies
Becoming symphonies
Perfume holding sway
As scent of cotton candy
           Faded
The piper blew his horn
We followed dancing
Tossing sparkles as confetti
Neverland disappearing
           Behind
Yet I have a secret
Map to hidden places
Where memories reside now
           Found

John Figurski, *Under Cover*

Ruth Zamoyta

Under the Blanket

They held the edges of their parents' blanket
(once a tent under which they played
with twiglike limbs and the milky breath of children)
and pulled it over their father's face.
Their mother sat in the corner picking at her chin,
knowing something bad had happened.
They got in their cars and drove home.

When the oldest got home, her lover woke up and they made love.
All night she lay still, listening to his breath,
avoiding his calloused heels and the damp patch on the sheets.

Zara Raab

Goldilocks

By all accounts, she was willful, yes, but
she often gave in—again and again,
she surrendered to siblings bigger or rougher.
Because she was pretty and blond,
some kids in adult dress found her charming.

By day, she wove filaments of light and bone
into a tousled shelter—charming!
There she slept on pillows of dry stone
flowing with milk and honey in her dreams.
Then one day it all changed—hence the story.

You know it well: How she goes in without
knocking and meets the bears who refuse her.
O, how the life she'd spread out before her
like a picnic blanket on the dull ground
steams then with her fright—and her fury!

Here's the sequel: next day or year she returns
and bleats like the lamb of old herdsmen
at their door, and yields up her pride
yet again to admit a deep bear love—
and then turns and sets out on her life.

Well, that was long ago and far away.
She's old now and sits on her heels
as day winds down like a goat stepping
in the dirt of rocky fissures, moving over
the mountain to the other side, into night.

Juyoung Yoo, *"Well, that was long ago and far away."*

Dawn Ferchak
"And the little one said..."

So they all rolled over and one fell out.

There were five in the bed and one blanket, and if one moved, they all moved and then something of someone's fell out.

A foot.
An arm.
A leg.
Some blanketless appendage, bare to the draft, with every turn, every night.

The little one was sly and small and always in the middle, in the spaces where there was blanket and pillow and the surrounding warmth of two bodies. Her siblings were heavy sleepers—until the draft was felt—and the little one could wriggle and burrow without waking anyone, if she found herself on an end.

There were always spaces to wriggle into, spaces between bodies that blamed each other for blanketless arms and legs and feet, and refused to touch even when dreaming.

On the coldest nights, the little one would whisper, "Roll over, roll over."

And they always would, and the blanket would roll with them, and someone's something would be left in the cold.

But not the little one, the wriggler warm and wee and wondering, always wondering why they always rolled Away and never Toward.

Toward the center
Toward the warmth
Toward a knot of family under the blanket large enough for them all.

Cecilia Oh, *"There were always spaces to wriggle into..."*

Enriqueta Carrington

On Stealing Figs

For my Tante Paulette

Time is suspended on the brink of fall
and I, a naughty child of five or six,
find sweet the fruit that grows beyond the wall.
My aunt is passionate about her figs
and in her garden forbidden trees sway
in the breeze, they whisper their calls, they tease,
(I must not) their honeyed globes on display,
(I will not) they wave their five-fingered leaves.
Flaunting their green swords, nasturtiums clamber,
each in its tunic the color of flame,
igniting the wall between, no barrier
for a sparrow, sparrow might be my name.
I fly into boughs that welcome, rock me,
I'm one of the songbirds, one with the tree.

I'm one of the songbirds, one with the tree,
all the flavors in the rainbow will burst
on my tongue, appease all hunger and thirst.
Shifting light, good rough bark between my knees,
the fig's weight in my hand, sun-warm, convex,
(there can be no world beyond this embrace)
gently bite, downy skin opens, displays
blushing globules round a shadowed vortex,
and there one eager drop. But that's no lark,
it's the woman of wrath, her trilling shriek.
She plucks me, shredding my skin on the bark
—I should have stayed high, but I was too meek—
she slaps me, shakes me till the world goes dark.
Is it next day, or the following week?

Is it next day, or the following week?
Again I hear the sinful call—it's wrong.
The spirit is willing, the flesh is strong,
though I was always taught to say it's weak.
At last, for love's own sake, I want to leave
the fruit untouched on other women's trees,
I tend the sweetest in my own garden.
Could I wing over the nasturtium wall
back into azure hours before the fall,
and in that garden undo one error,
I would be brave and challenge that terror,
woman who never had child or childhood.
I know I should not, but this time I would.

I know I should not, ah but yes, I would,
if there were one mistake that I could fix
 —I speak as one who's stolen many figs
and left too many things misunderstood—
as the fury dragged me from where I perched,
she'd put within my reach her chicken neck,
I'd grasp it firmly, and on her starved cheek
I'd plant one shameless, resounding, fruit-smirched…
She might rant, my great-aunt, and she might hiss
tes enfants, qu'ils sont terribles, horreur!
I never could resist forbidden figs,
though my thefts made trouble for my mother,
and in the end it all comes down to this:
plant one shameless, resounding, fruit-smirched kiss.

David Macpherson

The Five Senses at the Fair

There were five brothers who lived in the Morning Time under the blanket. The blanket was big and warm and felt like soft creation, but the brothers moved about so much, telling rude jokes and pulling stray hair, that they were never covered and they were cold. All five brothers said that it was the blanket's fault. The oldest brother, Taste, said, "I will go out and find something that will keep me warm." He left to work in a chili sauce factory as a quality tester, burning his mouth as much as he could. The second brother was Touch and he said, "This blanket is still a cold, short thing, I will go out to find warmth." He joined a sect that gives out literature on street corners and hugged tightly all those who allowed him, bleeding what heat he could from them. Brother Hearing did not even make his intention known. He just screamed at the top of his lungs and ran to catch the fleeing sound waves. He became employed at a shop that made customized emergency sirens. The fourth brother was Smell and he said, "If, with only two of us here under the blanket, I still cannot stay under, it is too small. I must go and be warm." He followed the scent of burning wood to campsites and worked as a forester. The last brother under the blanket was Sight and he knew it was time to go. He became an art critic and was warmed by disdain. All five brothers lived by themselves. All five brothers purchased thick blankets for their beds. All five brothers shivered into dawn. Years later and Taste went to an arts festival in the woods. He was selling his new hot sauce from the back of a van. The festival employed foresters to protect the setting and Smell was there. Touch's sect arrived to hand out literature. Sight was forced to attend by his editor, to write up a feature on the event. In the demonstration area, Hearing was showing off his new smoke alarm. He lit a fire and the technology blared and Smell came following the enticing odor of ash and Taste came because his booth was nearby and Touch followed the moving crowd, embracing whom he could, and Sight came because he thought this might be the next big art movement to explode. The five brothers saw each other and paused. They were remembering the Morning Time and the blanket. How it felt like grace. How it reeked of kindness. How it looked like arms embracing. How it rustled like movement slowing to sleep. How it tasted like summer nights. The five brothers. The blanket. The sense of this accord.

Juyoung Yoo, *"The blanket was big and warm and felt like soft creation..."*

Janelle Adsit

Introduction to World Peace, Course Final

after Conchitina Cruz

1.
a. in the power of willed wealth
b. in the power of wealth willed
c. in willpower
d. none of the above

2.
a. they had words for certainty
b. they had a sense for the sovereignty of dirt
c. they had an agreement that was actually a claim
d. they had the capacity for intended interruptions

3.
a. under the blanket, if they had not already been looking there
b. under the blanket, but they were uncomfortable beside each other
c. under the blanket, which was colored in a way they didn't like
d. under the blanket, since it couldn't be used for anything else

4.
a. by the car that would have caused the end
b. by the unused room that could have been
c. by the cafeteria that has been for quite some time
d. by the waiting room that would have to hide the empty syringe

5.
a. the argument wasn't worth having
b. the argument wasn't about having
c. the argument was that having is not worth much at all
d. the argument had something and therefore couldn't be what it was worth

6.
a. the blanket was all talk
b. the blanket was taken for granted
c. the blanket wasn't taken at all
d. the blanket was a type of token

7.
a. because no one could get outside to distribute it
b. because no one could feel the warmth
c. because the one outside would be the most and least powerful
d. because each body felt only its own heat

8.
a. no—or perhaps, according to familiarity
b. of course, like finding what would have, has been for quite some time
c. if so, despite the absence
d. maybe, if nothing more than nothing else

9.
a. from the gasoline can that would ignite
b. from the legal document that disclosed an error
c. from the inevitable boredom that the rope tries to stave off
d. from the mouth that could be pressed to the ground

10.
a. maybe tomorrow, or however long after, if we just
b. right this minute, if only we search high or low
c. it might be, if we keep up
d. none above

B. T. Joy

Our Vision

       it would seem then
that only our vision is to fault
       I'm thinking of the way
we stood together by the farm that day in Idaho
and how you missed the white ongoing show
of two Friesian horses on downtime in the fields
       how the female's swanny neck was sloughing
off every oyster of muscle threading the male's shoulders
       and all this observable from where we loitered
illuminated, as perfection is, by evening
       later, night-fire having seeped
down under the ocean of the clouds,
I asked you how you could have missed
those horses in their quiet field, playing at love,
       you answered by asking me
where *my* eyes had been
when the flowers of purple geraniums tipped
their shady, satin heads on the fence-posts there
       and how the subtle air
played too with their bodies
like playing at love
       it would seem then
that only our vision is to fault
that all we need is to stop this hauling back and forth;
       to centre ourselves in the eye of the other
       and it's only when pulling close to the beloved
that the lover sees the white-fronted geese
that ringed her garden as a child
       only when the beloved leans
on her lover's body that she senses, all at once,
the spring-air through his boyhood window
       I've heard it called *redemption, mercy, grace*
       and yes
coming together in this way is hard;
but not impossible

            tens-of-thousands died at Nagasaki
                    they say more are dying now; in the gentle
river-plains; the hills and yellow cities of Iraq
            and yet the global military budget
has reached 1.8
trillion dollars
            there has never been a better time
for verification
            for me seeing things as *you* do
            for climbing, as Rumi says,
up and down the pear tree
            for the eagle to seek, as Pawhuska says,
the deepest blue of the sky
            and please, don't misunderstand me
            this is not a wish
to see things as the heavens see them,
though partly that desire is there,
            but rather I want the man or woman
charged with dropping the bomb to see
            that every threadbare scrap of earth is full
of a thousand braces of Friesian horses
            of wire fences with no end;
laced and interlocked sublimely
            by the inward spiralling lines
of purple geraniums

Nicole Callihan

The Prayer

Midwinter, and I tuck my daughter in.
It's been dark for hours. She asks for a prayer.
I recite the only one I know, one I read in a book
In the months before she was born.
Dear Lord, I say, and she says it with me.
It seems the least I can do:
Give her something to believe in.
Outside the window, the moon is a tossed quarter.
Eva asks for water, for a kiss. Finally, a blanket.
By morning, she will have kicked it to the floor.

John Figurski, *The Sleeping Blonde*

Michael Smolinsky

To My Younger Brother at a Zen Monastery

We haven't spoken since you moved to Maine.
But I found this poem of mine from middle school
while cleaning out the old attic. Thought of you.

It's about a bird. Back then, I called it lame;
something's still wrong with the wing.
Do you think it will ever fly or sing?

We'd seen a bluebird from our bedroom window
almost every day that April—wounded, darting
back and forth in a pool of roots and rain.

Watching him, frantic, recalled your voice: *He got me!*
from the time I closed the car door on your thumb.
That breathless, staggered rhythm—

I don't know why I laughed.
You were in pain. Was I
cruel, anxious, caught off guard?

You never made a peep. At the dentist once,
the Novocaine faded and you accepted it in silence.
Accepted I would always be the favorite.

After I read the poem in class, I placed my ear on the cold
surface of the desk. It was like talking long distance on our
old rotary phone: sharp and static, broken full of emptiness.

Like laying my head on Dad's chest while he spoke,
just after his mother died. I was seven.
He was stoic. Mom was mute and still.

You went upstairs alone.

Rebecca Bersohn, *"Was I cruel, anxious, caught off guard?"*

Brittany Ericksen

Firstborn

But he shall acknowledge the firstborn, the son of the unloved, by giving him a double portion of all that he has, for he is the beginning of his strength; to him belongs the right of the firstborn.
—Deut. 21:17

This is my blanket, my birthright:
a modest inheritance
divided among siblings.
We collect memories like seashells,
we make our homes in tide pools
and watch tiny creatures pool at our feet
in silence. We will keep our secrets.

When will you learn? Your past is a gift
you cannot exchange.
I am my father's oldest child.
You can tell by our identical scars.

This is the blanket I share with my siblings.
It covers us, precariously.
We spend our lives trying to hold together
our legacy of scraps.
What do I have to give you?
I want you to have pristine sheets, immaculate.
I want to welcome you into my arms with perfection,
not my patchwork collection quilted with question marks,
the loose threads and ragged edges,
the inherent dissymmetry in its very fibers.
All these fragments,
this is what I own.

What will you inherit?
Your smile, a certain laugh, those unusual mannerisms—
the things that signal where we're from.
All those qualities I see in others, I envy,
that certain closeness, so thick you can wrap it around yourself.
It will keep you dry.

There are the things you inherit and the things you pass on.
I will build my estate from saltwater and shells.
You will have a room there, above the ocean
and we will watch the waves swallow up the shore.

Lois Marie Harrod

Barbara

I begged until my mother allowed me to go home
with Barbara, but not to stay overnight.

When we dropped from the school bus, Barbara's house—
not the big house with columns, *no, not there,*

but the unpainted shingle shack behind.
She got a cold ear of corn from the ice box

and offered it. The door shut gray.
Here's where we would have slept, she said,

pointing to a bruised bed with a thin blanket.
All of us together. Five sisters and Barbara and me.

Until supper, we wandered the estate—
barns, sheds, silos, fields, mud, runnels, streams—

until she lost her Goody hair barrette—a little thing.
We searched and walked, slopped and searched

and all the time she wept and wept.
I could not stop her weeping.

I said, *Ask your mother to buy another,*
but she just shook her head.

We were second-graders. I did not know
the price of things.

I thought of Barbara again when my son-in-law
left my daughter with a baby and a two-year-old

to sleep in another's bed. Her weeping. I thought about all
that could not be covered, could not be replaced.

Dawn Corrigan

The Pair Who Stayed

The man enters the house
with a tremendous banging

and hawking up phlegm.
He has a cold again.

He goes in the kitchen
and runs the water

at full power—
always full power—

and clatters the knives
in the sink

and rummages, loudly,
for something to eat.

Then he flings himself
into his seat,

turns on the TV
and flicks abruptly

from one station to another.
It's rude, I think,

cutting off so many speakers
mid-word.

Finally he clicks the power off
and tramples down the hall

to the bedroom.
He's my brother.

And only when
I hear him

murmuring to the cat
do I realize what

I meant to say:
Is your cold any better?

Did you have a nice time tonight?
How was your day?

John Figurski *Who's Driving?*

Nancy Cook

One Sixth

I am one
of six. Sisters.
Nine years, two
months between
oldest and
youngest.

I am one of
the six, fourth
from the top, third
from the bottom,
oldest of the
youngest—

that's how we
describe things. We live
two in Cleveland
one in Cincinnati,
one in Atlanta, one in
Arlington, Virginia,

and one west
of the Mississippi.
We're orphans,
our parents dead
twenty-eight and
thirty-seven summers.

Every year we
congregate
in our home town
after Christmas.
We spend
an afternoon

without children,
spouses banned,
just a few
bottles of wine and
everybody's best
baking. We laugh,

we tease,
we story tell,
we recollect
our mutual past,
the same,
but mostly different

in the ego-
centric plot of
memory. We
never speak
of pay raises,
promotions,

invitations,
kids' grades, trophies,
jackpots, pounds lost, golf
handicaps—anything
that might suggest
a betterness.

We laugh, we tease,
we downplay and
self deprecate.

But last year,
someone dared to ask
whom our parents

treasured most.
All agree
our mother had
no favorites and
all agree our father
did.

Six names
mentioned.
After much
animated con-
versation,
the consensus was

still too far away
to be discerned.
We would not
agree. So now
it seems that we
are guaranteed

to never know
who won.

Juditha Dowd

I Assume the Duties of the Eldest Child

Yes, she said. Take the portraits and pass them down—
to the *girls.* My mother and I were talking about the illness
that would be her last, but we ended up with laughter

as in former days when both of us were gayer. Laughed
till we were weak and teary, though I can't say what
was funny, just that all at once it was. That way of ours.

Half a century earlier she'd gone to save those portraits
when an uncle, short of funds, tried to hock them in Boston,
though they weren't her kin and my father had no interest.

But she was wrong about her sons—so wild and heedless
in our youth that many things of beauty had long since
been destroyed—belatedly they cared.

Gathering after the funeral to apportion what was left,
we made every item equal—teaspoon and trunk—breathed
a collective sigh as we slumped into battered chairs.

Sevres vases went to Steve, who declined the breakfront
so my daughter could fill it with her chipped plates.
We gave most of the rest to his twin, who feared the divvying

would turn nightmare, surrendered everything he wanted.
(It ended up in storage, as we knew it would.)
To my surprise, I needed little but the portraits, faces

of our history. I wandered empty rooms, found a bracelet
for a niece and sterling silver candlesticks for the house
she hoped to buy. My third brother, upset he'd forgotten

to consider her, began to weep. Then we were done, all
but the laughter, that way still ours. For an hour longer close
to what I imagine she'd wanted us to be.

Juyoung Yoo, "*Cut to measure, as a candy bar to kids . . .*"

Jacqueline Hughes Simon

Cut to Measure

No matter that love
is tendered equally,

Cut to measure,
as a candy bar to kids,

How the offer is
accepted   discarded,
postponed   refused,

Completes the dance
of memory   remorse.

Roslyn Tanner Evans

If Only

If only I were alone,
If only I had the bed to myself,
If only just one night,
If only, If only.

If only I were comfortable,
If only I were covered,
If only I were warm,
If only, If only.

If only my sisters hadn't heard me,
If only my brothers hadn't left,
If only I were not alone,
If only, If only.

If only they came back,
If only I said I was sorry,
If only we slept closer,
If only, If only.

Gail Denham

So Many Years

We drew a line down the bed's
middle. "Not one toe over the line,"
I told my sister. Cold nights, I reneged.

"And no more using my sweaters,"
I warned. Maybe I scared her. Who
knows? I wasn't a very good older

sister. Mean and didn't notice her
much. I regret that all days. She's
still my friend though. Amazing.

Yet, from the time I used to tell
her and little bro ghost stories,
(at their request), I did care,

just had trouble thinking past
my own troubles and happenings.
Then came children.

Our four sons, their friends;
all the fun, joy, trials, upsets.
Nothing better than snuggling

to read them a book at night,
or kiss them off to school
each day with a prayer.

After that, grandkids totally wiped
out personal absorption. It was all
for them, from day one, no question.

Strange it seems, it takes so many
years not to care about the line
down the middle, or sweaters.

Anne Harding Woodworth

Landays for a Drunk

after four siblings attempted to save the fifth

Old man, we found you comatose, near
death in dark piss and mice. You mumbled you were sleepy.

Best sleep's for lovers' restoration.
Your sleep pulled you down into lonely oblivion.

It's reptilian, this reaching for
vodka, *a force that through the green fuse drives the flower.*

Put your hat on, *homo sapiens*,
brim and crown, and protect your brain's regeneration.

Put your shoes on, *homo erectus*,
and walk out the door of your filthy cave forever.

Your legs are thin as bed slats. Who would
curl around them and on what blue-and-white striped ticking?

Sober you are haughty. You forget
by drinking your way into abject humility.

Worm, low as you are, you're not humble.
What makes you feel superior to nearby farmers?

Your wife left you with a bottle in
your mouth, infant boy she had put up for adoption.

It's safer to take a rescue dog
than an ashen pink sot with fur growing at the nape.

Moon has no hope of companionship,
yet it revels in contours, rebirth, and reflection.

May you soon be the moon, water to
sun's fire, ease in solitude, light rimming your head.

May you soon be the moon, travel great
heights, all-seeing, an owl, head orbiting on a branch.

Quote from Dylan Thomas, "The Force That through the Green Fuse Drives the Flower."

John Figurski, *The Wild Bunch*

John A. Vanek

Heavenly Father, help me

to remember that the blonde
who cut me off in traffic
and gave me the finger
may be on her ninth life
with a tomcat mate
and a litter of kids—

the dimwitted teen at McDonald's
who can't make change
and walks with a limp
is as fragile
as his shattered genes—

the thoughtless smoker
who second-handed me
probably can't think
of a way to tell his family
his biopsy was positive.

Help me to remember
that on the dark and foggy streets
of life, one careless turn
and you are on the corner with a sign,
asleep in a doorway,
lost forever—

that in the nowhereness
of anonymity, some folks
pawn their front-office dreams
for the back-alley oblivion
of the temporarily dead—

and Heavenly Father,
whenever I find someone's hope
dangling at the end of a noose,
help me get up off my knees,
sweep him into my arms
and lift just long enough
for him to cut the rope.

Juyoung Yoo, "*Help me get up off my knees, sweep him into my arms...*"

Isabalino Anastasio Guzman

My Grandfather's Blanket

To Jose Guzman

This winter my grandfather puts away the blanket,
graying into old photos—torn and worn by sleep.
He presses it to the ear in remembrance of siblings.
Listen, he says, *they play keep-away with my kaleidoscope.*
Turning a toothless grin, a sudden embrace cups
the gray fields over my head—they seem wet with tears.

I remember the stories of each tear,
the wars had for this one blanket.
And they would change with each cup
of coffee or tea: from Normandy-sleeps
to Cold War thievery—kaleidoscopes
to spy the changing brothers and sisters.

Near the end of each story, he interrupts: *No, it was my brother!*
Then second guesses. Repeats. Corrects again. Just to tear
away from his gaps. Mend the truth with fantasy—kaleidoscoping
the ruby autumn leaf with a budding broken branch. The blanket
rests as relic. A crown to earn. A dream forgetting to sleep.
But the real memories smudge at the bottom of his cup.

When grandpa isn't looking, I pick the grains from his cup.
To listen or taste them. To understand my own sibling
too far, too old, to hear or see sleep.
To understand the empty rooms fastened to our tears.
To remember and imagine moments being tucked in, my blanket
far too big. The details snap and twist in place—my own kaleidoscope.

And why do the colors change in memory? Why must kaleidoscopes
turn in silent heartbeats? Why and how do its mirrors cup
each secret in the infinite folds of each turn? Does this blanket
hold all my answers? *When I was ten there was a time my sister
buried it in the garden,* grandpa's eyes are wailing in tears,
to keep the seeds warm. To bring radiant dreams in frost-sleep.

And now it's time for it to sleep,
the job finally done. Wrapped in his old kaleidoscope,
he places it in a trunk—kissing the lid. Why do tears
drip and slide down our cheeks? Why must I cup
them to my mouth instinctively? It was a loss of a sibling,
several siblings, from the past and into our future—our blanket.

We will buy a new blanket, but continue our restless sleep.
I will think of my sister twisting in time's kaleidoscope.
I will cup my goodbyes. I will learn to shed those tears.

Rosemary O'Neil Wright

Harmony

We outgrew each other, planned our farewell.
Gus started singing, *Siblings of my heart
although we now must part.* No Bob Dylan
but I choked up. Until *Ten feet and fifty toes
travelin' along the roads.* I giggled
then wheezed. Smart mouth Richard
began, *Ten eyes and a thousand lashes
leading to a hundred clashes.* I howled.
In the heat of the moment I squeezed
Julie's hand, though we've had our
differences. I saw tears in her eyes
and all those lashes, started
to hiccup. Amy sang
This Little Light of Mine. Gus joined, then
Richard and I, even Julie, made up songs
kept going half the night.

So we started over, the five of us.
No bed of roses, not even daisies.
Gus snores, Richard drinks, Amy has nightmares.
Julie wants her Pekingese in bed. Sometimes
I think I'll scream. Then somebody starts
to sing.

Rebecca Bersohn, "*Then somebody starts to sing.*"

Sherri Lynn Cooper

The Blanket

Forty little fingers, ten thumbs and fifty toes.
All in random order and none are in neat rows.
Everybody squirming, yes sir, the fight is on!
No one there to settle it with Mom and Dad both gone.
Two pull the blanket to the left, three scream and pull it right.
Yes, this gorgeous blanket is causing quite the fight.
Nobody is covered, part of everyone is bare.
Oh, how this day would differ if Mom or Dad were there.
"My feet are frozen solid," screams Sammy from the end.
"Well, maybe we could fit us all if Mikey wouldn't bend."
"Well, Julie's feet are on my back and I am going to yell."
"And Jimmy will not tattle, 'cause there is no one to tell."
And Jordan starts to cry a bit, he's cold and getting tired.
While all the others scream and yell, oh man these kids are wired.
And finally the oldest boys decide they've had enough.
Five kids with just one blanket, this night is getting rough.
So Jim and Mike hop out of bed, a blanket they will find.
The other three are finally warm, so this they do not mind.
They cannot find another, though they look for half an hour.
And when they get back to the room, the other kids look sour.
Now Jimmy knows this will not work, the same way as before.
Five kids and just one blanket, a bed and nothing more.
He says, "I am the oldest, so what I say must go.
Now everybody out of bed, we must lie in a row."
So all the children scurry to do what Jimmy said.
Now everyone is in a row and fitting in the bed.
Then Jimmy takes the blanket off and puts it down once more.
And everyone is covered, with the blanket to the floor.
"Thank you Jimmy," Jordan says "I'm glad you are the oldest."
"No problem," Jimmy says with pride, "I'm sure you were the coldest."
Forty little fingers, ten thumbs and fifty toes, everybody toasty lying neatly in a row.

Judith McNally

Blanket

A   Remember how we used to fight over that blanket?

B   I do. The five of us pulling and tussling, trying to get warm.

A   Jesse used to ball up a corner of it and clamp down with her teeth. I thought she'd never let go.

B   And what about *you*?

A   What about me?

B   You used to grab the side with both hands and hold on so tight that blanket was in shreds.

A   I did?

B   And you were the oldest of the five, too. What kind of example was that?

A   Like you said, just trying to keep warm. And Anna Marie, with her little feet sticking out.

B   Good thing for all of us I had the big idea that one night—remember there were icicles *inside* the windows?

A   I thought it was Jesse's idea.

B   No, it was mine.

A   Couldn't have been. You could barely talk yet, then.

B   That's why it was me. I had this idea, and I started grabbing for each of you, bringing you all closer and closer together until we were all in the middle. One big huddle underneath the blanket. One big *warm* huddle.

A   An idea put into motion, instead of words.

B   It was either that, or—

A   —Or what?

B   What Mom and Dad used to call blanket punishment.

Juyoung Yoo, "*All we can do is hang on to our pendulum . . .*"

Manhattanpoet

The Blanket

Strange as it may sound
The blanket fits our string theory
Whitehead's process and reality
And very deep at the core of its heat
Descartes' doubt
Whether we exist

We're under something
That much we know
Sometimes comforting, sometimes asphyxiating
All we can do
Is hang on to our pendulum
And favor the swing

Every peak has its abyss

We *are* the blanket.

Lisa Lebduska

Butterfly Sleep

Burst from pearls, sibling worms
Argue the universe verdant, spinning
The long nap
That erupts us
Into floating lemon leaves
Ambrosiaed,
We drowse heavy
Nectar dreams
Of our flights
Tightly folded
Days of drinking
Air and perfume
Pendulous rich
Tang in our dance.
Why battle?
Dew lives evaporate in the heat of a morning
That never lasts but always returns
As sure as blossoms.

Cecilia Oh, *"The long nap that erupts us..."*

Sharon Olson

Looking for My Other Brother

He used to be our middle brother
but somehow he got away, and even though
the money allotted to us was the same,
for him it was not enough

I use Google Earth to find him now,
navigating the streets of Las Vegas
where his home was foreclosed,
just another happening he never
disclosed to us

I visited him there once—the lost home,
beige like all the other ones on the street—
on a three-hour Southwest Airlines stopover,
stepping past occasional furniture I didn't
recognize to have lunch with him
at a Formica table. We talked about
everything but money, a promise
we had made at the airport

One of his postcards mentioned an address
that puts him snug between KFC and the Nevada
School of Massage. I imagine him comforted by
those sticky chicken legs and the oil they use
for cooking them, not unlike what is rubbed
into one's skin before the masseuse begins—
make yourself comfortable—she invariably says

On Google's street view I scan the perimeter
of pseudo-abobe apartment walls, looking for Mother's
old Cadillac in the parking lot—he'd be lucky to keep it
running. He works hard, he says, dancing all night
with women one third his age. At seventy he still
has the moves   the shuffle   the dip
the quick duck out of sight

Carolyn Faye Davis

The Blanket

At first, the blanket was enough.
Bequeathed to all five sons as one,
it was sewn from bits of each boy's clothes
and held the history of their lives.

That first night, they all piled in Grossmutter's bed
and pulled the new coverlet over their knees.
Propping on pillows and leaning on Simon,
the littler ones listened to him tell their stories,
each tale reflected in swatches of fabric.
The squares in the corners were Fabio's t-shirt,
Sebastian's pajamas formed stripes down the long side,
the border itself came from Oliver's socks,
and Leo's bright flannels were appliquéd rainbows.
They cuddled together beneath the warm colors,
a quintet of boys falling tandem to sleep.

But, in the night, the room grew cold
and one by one the brothers woke
and yanked the blanket back and forth
to claim its favors for himself.

Each boy forgot so soon
the warmth he found enclosed
in his brothers' open arms,

and the room without
turned only colder

and distant.

Juyoung Yoo, "*In tattered clothes be our garment.*"

Basil Rouskas

Shared Blanket

In tattered clothes
be our garment.

Cover our bed
when we need sleep.

Keep the good
dreams in the room.

Trust us to share fairly
this earth's frail blanket.

Amen!

Poets

Janelle Adsit's poetry, book reviews, and essays appear in publications such as *Confrontation, Caketrain, Mid-American Review, Colorado Review,* and *ForeWord*. She is a doctoral candidate in the English program at SUNY Albany where she teaches creative writing.

Austin Alexis won the 20th annual Naomi Long Madgett Poetry Award for his first full-length collection, *Privacy Issues* (Lotus Press). His second chapbook, *For Lincoln & Other Poems* (Poets Wear Prada), was a *Small Press Review* "Pick of the Month." His poetry has appeared in anthologies such as *Off the Cuffs: Poetry by and about the Police* (Soft Skull Press), *Empty Shoes: Poems on the Hungry and the Homeless* (Popcorn Press), and *Rabbit Ears: TV Poems* (Poets Wear Prada). He has work forthcoming in *Home Planet News* and *Poetry Pacific* (Canada). He has taught at Hunter College and in an NEA-funded program for the Jamaica Center for Arts and Learning in Queens, NY.

Jennifer Arin is the author of the poetry collection *Ways We Hold* (2012), and her writings have been published in both the U.S. and Europe, including in *The AWP Writer's Chronicle, The San Francisco Chronicle Sunday Book Review, Gastronomica, Puerto del Sol, Poet Lore, ZYZZYVA, Chain, Paris/Atlantic Review,* and *The Chronicle of Higher Education,* among others. Recent awards include a grant from the National Endowment for the Humanities, a PEN Writer's Fund grant, a Poets & Writers Writers-On-Site Residency, and funding from the Spanish Ministry of Culture. She teaches in the English Department at San Francisco State University.

Rev. Dr. David Breeden has a Master of Fine Arts degree in poetry from the Iowa Writers' Workshop and a PhD from the Center for Writers at the University of Southern Mississippi, with additional study in writing and Buddhism at Naropa Institute in Boulder, Colorado. He also has a Master of Divinity degree from Meadville Lombard Theological School. Breeden has published four novels and thirteen books of poetry, the newest titled *They Played for Timelessness (With Chips of When)*.

Nicole Callihan writes poems, stories, and essays. Her work has appeared in, among others, *The L Magazine, Cream City Review, Forklift, Ohio,* and *Painted Bride Quarterly*. Her books include the 2012 nonfiction *Henry River Mill Village,* a documentation of the rise and fall of a tiny mill village turned ghost town in North Carolina, which she co-wrote with Ruby Young Keller; as well as *SuperLoop,* a collection of poems published by Sock

Poets

Monkey Press in early 2014. She teaches at NYU and lives in Brooklyn where she cuddles under a blanket with her husband and daughters.

Enriqueta Carrington's poetry in Spanish and English has appeared in *U.S. 1 Worksheets, 14 by 14, Lighten Up Online, The Shit Creek Review, The Chimaera*, and *Contemporary Sonnet*, among other journals, and has received the *Atlanta Journal's* International Merit Award. Her poetry translations from the Spanish have appeared in *The New Formalist, Rattapallax*, and *A Gathering of the Tribes*, among other journals. Her translations from the Sicilian have appeared in *Descant* (Canada). She is the translator of several volumes of poetry, including *Treasury of Mexican Love Poems* (Hippocrene Books) and *Samandar: Libro de Viajes/Book of Travels*, by Lourdes Vázquez (Editorial Tsé-Tsé, Argentina). She is one of the poetry editors for the journal *U.S. 1 Worksheets*. She holds a PhD in mathematics from Rutgers University, and taught for many years at the National University of Mexico, the University of California at Berkeley, Temple University, and Rutgers University. In September 2013 she retired from mathematics to become a full-time translator and writer.

Nancy Cook is one of six sisters and a parent, lawyer, teacher, and writer living in St. Paul, Minnesota. Her work has most recently appeared in *Adventum, Eleventh Muse, The Rust Belt Rising Almanac*, and the anthology, *Poet's Quest for God*. With the help of an Artists Initiative grant from the Minnesota State Arts Board, Nancy is currently coordinating a series of community justice-writing workshops, the goal of which is to enable the narrative development and dissemination of stories of, by, and for populations underserved by the justice system.

Sherri Lynn Cooper lives in the small town of Watson, Saskatchewan with her six children and husband. She is the second oldest of eight children. She was raised by her amazing mother and father who are both still alive and well. She has lived everywhere from Lake Placid, New York, to Madoc, Ontario. She loves writing, rhyming, and gardening in her spare time. Her favorite children's authors are Robert Munsch and Dr. Seuss. She has recently started entering poetry contests and finds it very relaxing. She hopes when all of her children are grown she will be able to find more writing time.

Dawn Corrigan's poetry and prose have appeared in a number of print and online journals, most recently *DIALOGIST, So to Speak, Digital Americana, egg*, and *The New Verse News*. She lives in Gulf Breeze, Florida.

Carolyn Faye Davis's early life was spent in schools and universities—18 years as a full-time student—and was such a wonderful experience that she really didn't want to leave academia. Along the way, though, she earned Bachelor of Science and Master of Science degrees in biology, a Bachelor of Science degree in Electrical Engineering, and certification in Advanced Studies in Higher Education. After a career as a teacher, engineer, and nonprofit association director, she is now a poet-in-progress, occasionally seeing her poems published or winning an award. She currently lives, with her husband, in the Smoky Mountains of North Carolina, where she is hard at work on a chapbook of Appalachian poetry.

For some 35 years, **Gail Denham's** poetry, short stories, essays, news articles, and photos have appeared in a variety of publications. Presently, Denham's focus is poetry and flash fiction; her main subjects are humor, family, and story. Since digital photography took over, Denham is slowly transferring her still photos to disc. Denham clearly remembers sharing a bed with her sister.

Juditha Dowd's poetry has been published in many journals, featured on Poetry Daily, and nominated for a Pushcart Prize. Her latest collection is *Mango in Winter* (Grayson Books, 2013). She has been awarded fellowships at Virginia Center for the Creative Arts and Vermont Studio Center and has previously published three chapbooks. A poetry editor for *U.S. 1 Worksheets*, she belongs to Cool Women, a poetry performance ensemble based in Princeton, New Jersey.

Brittany Ericksen is a crime victims' attorney living and working in the District of Columbia. She graduated from the Evergreen State College in Olympia, Washington, with a BA in English. She enjoys vegan cooking, Japanese fashion, and comic books.

Dawn Ferchak has been writing since she could hold a crayon in her fat baby hand. While she has moved on from Crayola poems about her pet cat, she remains content with living inside her own head, which is densely populated and has bits that are always on fire. She reviews books at BookshelfBombshells.com and promises to update her blog, www.wordsbydawn.com.

Ellen Foos is a senior production editor for Princeton University Press. She is the founder and publisher of Ragged Sky Press and was the recipient of a

Poets

fellowship to the MacDowell Colony and the Vermont Studio Center. Her first collection of poems, *Little Knitted Sister*, was published in 2006 and her poetry has appeared in *U.S.1 Worksheets, The Kelsey Review, Edison Literary Review,* and *Sensations Magazine.*

Isabalino Anastasio Guzman is a poet and student. His main goal is to explore the multiplicity of language and society through the surrealistic use of imagery. He is currently near completion of his first chapbook, a book exploring the ideas of Italian writer Italo Calvino. Isabalino has been published in over a dozen publications including: *Big City Lit, The Same Magazine, Shot Glass Journal, Symmetry Pebbles, Underground Voices,* and *Toe Good Poetry*. He has also been featured several times at various reading series at the Cornelia Street Café in Manhattan. In 2011 he was given the Award for Outstanding Achievement in Creative Writing at LaGuardia Community College. He hopes, by the end of 2014, to have his first collection published.

Anne Harding Woodworth is the author of four books of poetry and two chapbooks. Her poetry, essays, and book reviews are published widely in literary journals in print and online. She spent her childhood on a farm in New York State with her four siblings, who are often a source—and a rich one—for her writing. She now divides her time between the mountains of North Carolina and Washington, D.C., where she is a member of the Poetry Board at the Folger Shakespeare Library.

Lois Marie Harrod's 13th poetry collection, *Fragments from the Biography of Nemesis*, has just been published by Word Tech (Cherry Grove). *The Only Is* won the 2012 Tennessee Chapbook Contest (*Poems & Plays*), and *Brief Term*, a collection of poems about teachers and teaching, was published by Black Buzzard Press, 2011. *Cosmogony* won the 2010 Hazel Lipa Chapbook Contest (Iowa State). She is widely published in literary journals and online e-zines from *American Poetry Review* to *Zone 3*. She teaches Creative Writing at The College of New Jersey. Read her work on loismarieharrod.com.

Jacqueline Hughes Simon earned her BA from Berkeley having returned to university after raising two daughters. At Berkeley she studied poetry with John Shoptaw and Robert Hass. She received the 2013 Judith Lee Stronach re-entry prize for poetry. Her work has been published in the *Cal Literature & Arts Magazine (CLAM).*

B.T. Joy is a Glaswegian poet who currently lives in Bridge of Weir, Renfrewshire, where he teaches High School English. Between 2006 and 2009 he lived in London where he studied and mentored at London Metropolitan University, gaining a First Class Honours degree in Creative Writing and Film Studies. Since then he has had poetry and fiction published in American, Australian, Irish, Japanese, Hongkongese, and British magazines, journals, and anthologies. In 2012 he was nominated for the Ravenglass Poetry Press Competition judged by the Dundonian poet Don Paterson.

In 2014 **Dean Kostos's** book, *This Is Not a Skyscraper*, won the Benjamin Saltman Poetry Award, selected by Mark Doty. It will be published by Red Hen Press in March of 2015. Kostos is the author of the following collections: *Rivering, Last Supper of the Senses, The Sentence That Ends with a Comma*, and *Celestial Rust*. He was also the coeditor of *Mama's Boy: Gay Men Write about Their Mothers* (a Lambda Book Award finalist) and the editor of *Pomegranate Seeds: An Anthology of Greek-American Poetry*. His poems, personal essays, and reviews have appeared in *Barrow Street, Boulevard, Chelsea, Cimarron Review, New Madrid, Southwest Review, Stand Magazine, Talisman, Western Humanities Review*, on Oprah Winfrey's Web site oxygen.com, the Harvard University Press website, and in many other leading journals. His poem "Subway Silk" was adapted into a film by Canadian filmmaker Jill Clark.

Lisa Lebduska teaches writing and directs the college writing program at Wheaton College in Massachusetts. Her work has appeared in such publications as *Writing on the Edge, The Providence Journal, Narrative*, and the audio magazine *4'33"*. Born in Brooklyn, she visits often and listens but never hears quite as much as she would like.

David Macpherson is a writer living in Central Massachusetts with his wife, Heather, and son, George. He is the host of the Hangover Hour Spoken Word Salon held twice a month in Worcester. He has been published in *Every Day Fiction, Haggard and Halloo*, and *Mudluschious*, among other places.

Manhattanpoet See **Paulina Rieloff-Nielsen**, on page 68.

Judith McNally is the author of *Jigsaw*, a first novel, and *CHOPPING without CHOPPING*, a collection of micro-dialogues. She is the recipient of a New

Poets

Jersey State Council on the Arts Prose Fellowship, and her one-man play, *Birdland*, was optioned by The New Federal Theatre, New York City. Over a 20-year period, Judith has taught creative writing at City College of New York, to adults at Mercer County Community College, plus at numerous high school residencies and Teen Arts Festivals through the New Jersey School for the Arts. Her dialogues and poems have appeared in many issues of *U.S.1 Worksheets*. Currently she is at work on a project combining music and words.

Susan Laughter Meyers of Givhans, South Carolina, is the author of *My Dear, Dear Stagger Grass*, inaugural winner of the Cider Press Review Editors Prize. Her collection, *Keep and Give Away* (University of South Carolina Press), won the SC Poetry Book Prize and a SIBA Book Award. Her work has also appeared in numerous journals and anthologies, including *The Southern Review, Prairie Schooner,* and *Crazyhorse*.

Sharon Olson is a native-born Californian who worked as a librarian for the Palo Alto City Library for 29 years until she retired in 2007. After four years in Connecticut, she moved to Lawrenceville, NJ. She earned a BA in Art History from Stanford and attended its campus in Florence, Italy, in 1967. She also has an MLS from UC Berkeley and an MA in Comparative Literature from the University of Oregon. Her book of poems, *The Long Night of Flying*, was published by Sixteen Rivers Press in 2006. Her work has appeared in such journals as *The Arroyo Literary Review, U.S. 1 Worksheets,* and *Cider Press Review*, which nominated one of her poems for a Pushcart Prize.

Zara Raab's poems evoke the rainy darkness of the remote northern California coast where her family has lived for almost two hundred years. The poems are collected in *The Book of Gretel* and *Swimming the Eel*, and now in a third book, *Fracas and Asylum*, which continues her journey through inner and outer landscapes characterized by alternating moods of storm, seclusion, and reverie. A fourth book, finalist for the Dana Award and based on the tale of Rumpelstiltskin, will appear later this year. Raab's poems, reviews, and essays appear in *Evansville Review, River Styx, Crab Orchard Review, The Dark Horse,* and *Poet Lore*. A contributing editor for Redwood Coast Review and Poetry Flash, she lives near the San Francisco Bay.

Paulina Rieloff-Nielsen (Manhattanpoet) was born in Santiago de Chile. She traveled to the United States and has lived in New York City for the last 50 years. She briefly attended Columbia University's School of General Studies and ultimately graduated from Hunter College. In 1986 she made a poetry chapbook, *The Manhattanpoet*. Her work has been published in the *Revista de la Academia* at Hunter College's Romance Languages Department. She has participated in poetry readings at the Nuyorican Poets Café in Alphabet City, St. Mark's Church, and West Village coffee houses. She is the founder of The Paulina Rieloff Center for Global Cultural Expression Art Gallery.

Basil Rouskas is the author of two poetry collections: *Redrawing Borders* and *Blue Heron on Black River*, both by Finishing Line Press. A third book of his, *The Window That Faces South*, was quarter finalist in the third (2014) Mary Ballard Poetry Chapbook Prize by Casey Shay Press. His poetry has also appeared in Diane Lockward's 2013 book *The Crafty Poet: A Portable Workshop*. Basil's poetry has been featured in many poetry venues (print and online) including *The New York Times,* Princeton Public Library podcasts, *Exit 13, Illuminations,* and *Tiferet: A Journal of Spiritual Literature.* Basil has worked in corporate and not-for-profit organizations in the roles of executive, entrepreneur, consultant, and leadership coach. He has also taught at leading universities on leadership development, personal strength assessment, and team effectiveness.

Michael Smolinsky is an MFA candidate at Rutgers-Newark. He lives in Brooklyn, NY.

As far as **Roslyn Tanner Evans** can remember, she always wrote in rhyme. She joined a group of friends who wrote, some seriously, and over the past 15 years Roslyn stretched her writing skills and no longer has to rhyme. She never knew herself to be creative—certainly not artistic—until, upon retirement, she unexpectedly became a jewelry entrepreneur. A class in beading opened up a new world of beauty and creativity, and her business was born. It evolved into a dynamic mother/daughter team that crafts handmade jewelry inspired by nature. She reinvented herself through social media marketing at the age of 72. She now knows herself to be artistic and creative, and she looks forward to spending the remainder of her life expressing herself through words and beads.

Maria Terrone is the author of the poetry collections *A Secret Room in Fall* (McGovern Award, Ashland Poetry Press) and *The Bodies We Were Loaned* (The Word Works), as well as a chapbook, *American Gothic, Take*

Poets

2 (Finishing Line Press). Her third collection, *Eye to Eye*, is forthcoming from Bordighera Press in 2014. Her work, which has been translated into French and Farsi and nominated four times for a Pushcart Award, has appeared in magazines including *Poetry, Ploughshares, Hudson Review*, and *Poetry International*, and in 20 anthologies. She was one of ten Queens-based writers commissioned in Spring 2012 by the Guggenheim Museum for its project, "sillspotting nyc." Read more about Maria and her poems at mariaterrone.com.

John A. Vanek is a physician and poet with works published in numerous literary journals and showcased on public radio. He has read his poetry at the George Bush Presidential Library, the Akron Art Museum, Eckerd College, and the Cleveland Clinic. His book, *Heart Murmurs: Poems*, is available at Amazon.com

Christopher Woods is a writer, teacher, and photographer who lives in Texas. Among his published works are a prose collection, *Under a Riverbed Sky*, and a book of stage monologues for actors, *Heart Speak*. His photographs can be seen in his gallery: christopherwoods.zenfolio.com.

While in high school **Rosemary O'Neil Wright** read a quote from Dylan Thomas, "Poetry is not the same as prayer, but it arises from the same need." The words resonated with her and she has been reading poetry ever since. Rosemary earned an MA in Education from Stanford University and taught high school mathematics for twenty years. After her retirement she began taking writing classes at Brookdale Community College where she had several poems published in the literary magazine. Rosemary is now enrolled in the Monmouth University MA program in Creative Writing. Rosemary has also been a professional storyteller for over twenty-five years. She performs at festivals, banquets, and libraries. She is a member of the Garden State Storytellers League and the New Jersey Storytelling Network, and has organized a new group of storytellers at the Jersey Shore called Storytellers Mosaic.

Michelle Young attended the University of Tennessee at Chattanooga, and currently lives in Chattanooga with her husband, Corey Green. She is a professional singer, songwriter, and vocal instructor who has recorded and toured in Europe as well as North America. She has had work published in *The Sequoyah Review, Electronic Musician Magazine*, and *Songs and Hymns for Him*. She has also been featured in several magazines such as *iO Pages* (Holland), *Empire Magazine* (Germany), *Harmonie Magazine* (France), and *Progression Magazine* (USA), along with inclusion in *The Billboard Guide to Progressive Music.* Michelle is currently a member of the Chattanooga Writers' Guild and the National Association of Photoshop Professionals.

Ruth Zamoyta, co-editor of *Blanket Stories*, is also is the author of *'Otsu' and Other Poems* (2007, Bronze by Gold) and *clarissa@loveless.com* (2002, classicnovels.com), and the co-editor, with Ellen Foos and Vasiliki Katsarou, of *Eating Her Wedding Dress: A Collection of Clothing Poems* (2009, Ragged Sky), which features her poem, "My Bra." She lives in the New York City area where she develops strategies and runs projects for arts and education non-profits by day, and fences épée by night.

Artists

Rebecca Bersohn, as an artist, is interested in creating pop art that jumbles nostalgia, reality, and memory through juxtapositions, morphings, and collections of images and objects that seem visually important and/or humorous to her. Right now she is interested in mid-century modern furniture and placing it in contexts where it does not belong.

John Figurski was born and raised in New York City and earned a BFA in Art Education at SUNY New Paltz. He has lived in Manhattan since 1974 paying the rent and having fun as an illustrator and graphic designer. Various clients include *Heavy Metal*, *Cosmopolitan*, *National Lampoon*, and *Avenue* magazines; Time Inc.; Edelman Public Relations Worldwide; The Condé Nast Publications; Hearst Corporation; AT&T; and Polydor Records. In his spare time he enjoys playing poker, watching black & white movies, and getting lost in Manhattan.

Cecilia Oh was born and raised in Los Angeles, CA, and moved to New York City to earn her BFA in Communications Design at Pratt Institute. After her graduation in 2013, she immediately found her passion in teaching and she is now attending Teachers College, Columbia University in the Art and Art Education program. Since she has found a new love and respect for teaching, she uses art as a form of communication and expression within the classroom. She hopes to continue her own works of art as she becomes an educator who facilitates a rich experience for her students.

Juyoung Yoo, after earning Bachelor of Fine Arts and Master of Fine Arts in Sculpture from Seoul National University, moved to New York and attended Teachers College, Columbia University, to study art education. Living in New York and studying art education inspired her to create illustrative paintings often related to art museums. She currently lives and works in New York to continue making art, to share thoughts about art with others, and to find and produce written supports for what she does with art.

Acknowledgments

We would like to thank Judith M. Burton, Professor of Art Education at Teachers College, Columbia University; the Art and Art Education Program at Teachers College; the Macy Art Gallery; and the Myers Foundation for their support of this project. A very special thanks to John Figurski for the design of the cover and interior of this book, and to Dorothea Lasky for encapsulating the "heart of the blanket" in her introduction. Thanks to Ellen Foos, Nicholas ("Nick") Beatty and Amanda Kusek for lending their editorial expertise, and again to Nick for helping "spread the blanket" through social media. And, because this book is only one patch in a larger quilt, we extend our thanks to all involved with the other pieces of the larger Blanket Stories project: to Ann Teed for managing the visual art contributions and planning the exhibit, to all the teachers who encouraged their students to contribute to Blanket Stories and aided them in production, to Jeanne Goffi-Fynn for managing musical contributions, and to Trina Robinson for designing the website. Above all, our gratitude to all the poets, artists, and musicians who listened to the Blanket Story, felt something, and shared their feelings with the world through their art.

Now it's your turn!

Join the **Blanket Stories** collaboration by sending us your own creative response. We will post your creation in our online gallery, so if you'd like to get credit, please make sure to write your name and email address clearly.

Email your work to: **poetry@blanketstories.net**

Or mail to: **Blanket Stories**
c/o Professor Richard Jochum
Box 78, Teachers College • Columbia University
525 West 120th Street • New York, NY 10027

Visit us at: **blanketstories.net**
Like us on Facebook:
facebook.com/theblanketstoriesproject

www.ingramcontent.com/pod-product-compliance
Lightning Source LLC
Chambersburg PA
CBHW041523090426
42737CB00038B/104